$IX FIGURES IN 12 MONTHS

SIX FIGURES IN 12 MONTHS

$IX FIGURES IN 12 MONTHS

HOW I BUILT A SIX FIGURE LIFE INSURANCE BUSINESS USING SOCIAL MEDIA & HOW YOU CAN TOO

Success blueprint for new and existing life insurance agents, and digital marketing strategies used by the top agents in the financial industry

DIPO ADESINA

SIX FIGURES IN 12 MONTHS

COPYRIGHT PROTECTION

If you have purchased this book without proper authorization or from an unofficial source, please be aware that neither SADA Global Financial, nor its employees or agents, have received any payment for the copy. Counterfeit books can contribute to illicit activities, and it's illegal. We urge you not to purchase unauthorized copies and to report any instances of counterfeit distribution to SADA Global Financial.

This publication aims to provide accurate and reliable information related to the subject matter covered. However, it is sold with the understanding that neither the author nor SADA Global Financial is engaged in rendering legal, financial, or other professional services. Laws and practices differ across jurisdictions; if you require legal or other professional advice, we recommend consulting a qualified expert. The author and SADA Global Financial disclaim any liability arising from the use or application of the contents of this book.

Copyright © 2024 by SADA Global Financial. All rights reserved. Except as permitted under the U.S. Copyright Act of 1976, no part of this publication may be reproduced, distributed, or transmitted in any form or by any means, or stored in a database or retrieval system, without prior written permission from the publisher.

SADA Global Financial
10451 Mill Run Circle, Suite 400
Owings Mills, MD, 21117

Disclaimer: The information presented in this book is intended for informational purposes only. While every effort has been made to ensure accuracy and currency, neither the author nor SADA Global Financial assumes responsibility for any errors or omissions. No liability is assumed for incidental or consequential damages in connection with or arising from the use of the information contained herein.

Published in the United States
First Printing, 2024

Dedication

I dedicate this book to God, whose guidance and wisdom have enabled the success I've experienced on my journey in the financial industry. Each day, I prayed a simple prayer: "God, do something in my business that it will be impossible for me to take the glory for it." This book and the accomplishments it reflects are the answer to that prayer.

SIX FIGURES IN 12 MONTHS

Contents

INTRODUCTION

From Zero to Six Figures 1

CHAPTER 1

The Foundation of Success 7

CHAPTER 2

Mastering the Basics of Life Insurance: Carving Out Your Expertise 15

CHAPTER 3

The Money Is In the Niches 23

CHAPTER 4

Social Media Strategies for Growth 29

CHAPTER 5

Attraction Marketing: Creating Engaging Content That Sells 39

CHAPTER 6

Beyond the Basics: Building a Magnetic Personal Brand in Financial Services 47

CHAPTER 7

Increase Sales by 10X: Setting Up Automation and Systems 55

CHAPTER 8

Facebook and Instagram Ads—How to Generate Qualified Leads 24/7 67

CHAPTER 9
Triple Your Income with a Higher Comp 75
CHAPTER 10
Make Money First, Then Recruit 83
CHAPTER 11
How to Stay Ahead of the Competition 91
CHAPTER 12
Imitate the Top 10% of Agents 99

SIX FIGURES IN 12 MONTHS

SIX FIGURES IN 12 MONTHS

INTRODUCTION

From Zero to Six Figures

My Transformation into a Top-Earning Life Insurance Agent

What if you could transform a struggling life insurance business into a six-figure success in a single year? Imagine having the tools to do just that—despite starting from scratch in a crowded industry with well-worn, outdated strategies that seem to help everyone but you. When I began my journey as a life insurance agent, I was at a crossroads between that traditional path and a new, digital-first world waiting to be explored.

Like so many new agents, I started out the old-fashioned way: lists of family and friends, attending networking events, and back-to-back Zoom calls that went nowhere. My early days were, frankly, discouraging. For six months, I barely kept my head above water—my only initial policies were for my immediate family. But after seeing my meager commissions, I knew I had to either find a breakthrough or face burnout.

Then I made a pivotal decision: I would redefine my approach and harness the power of digital marketing to engage with clients on their terms. In December 2021, I launched my first TikTok video on life insurance. To my shock, it received over 41,000 views in one day—and that was just the beginning. That first video eventually grew to over 561,000 views, marking the turning point in my career. From then on, I was no longer "chasing" clients. Instead, they were coming to me, eager to learn about securing their family's future.

By the end of my first year, my business had skyrocketed to nearly $400,000—a feat I achieved through the power of social media, engaging content, and a digital approach that resonated with today's consumer.

The Problem Facing Agents Today

If you're reading this, you're probably a life insurance agent looking for growth in a challenging and rapidly changing market. You may have a book of tired methods: cold calling, endless networking, friends and family, and unpredictable referrals. The question is: are these strategies bringing the results you want? Or do they feel outdated, more frustrating than fruitful?

The hard truth is that consumer behavior has changed dramatically. People no longer respond to hard-sell tactics; they're seeking information, guidance, and engagement—especially online. Social media platforms are where buying decisions are being made, not at networking luncheons or through cold calls. Yet, despite this shift, many agents remain trapped in the past, losing the chance to connect with clients who are actively searching for financial insights online.

A Digital Blueprint for Success

This book is your guide to breaking free from ineffective methods and building a thriving business in the digital age. I'll walk you through the exact blueprint that helped me achieve six-figure success, from creating an engaging online presence to automating lead generation so you can focus on what matters most: serving your clients.

Here's what you'll gain from this book:

- **Building a Strong Foundation**: Learn how to set clear goals, master product knowledge, and build trust with a client-first approach.

- **Mastering Digital Marketing**: Discover the strategies for generating leads through a dynamic online presence and scalable social media ads.

- **Leveraging Social Media for Growth**: Gain insight into creating educational, authentic content that resonates with today's consumers.

- **Automating for Efficiency**: Explore marketing and automation techniques to nurture leads and boost conversions while freeing up your time.

Why This Book Stands Out

Unlike traditional sales guides, this book doesn't offer vague advice or recycled techniques. *Every strategy here is battle-tested and designed for a digital-first world.* I won't ask you to "make more calls" or "work harder"—instead, I'll show you how to work smarter by leveraging proven digital tools that can revolutionize your business.

This is not about discarding all that you know. It's about enhancing what you do with powerful digital techniques that make your business both scalable and sustainable, turning you into a sought-after expert in the field.

Who This Book Is For

This book is designed for:
- **New agents** struggling to build momentum in a highly competitive industry.

- **Experienced agents** seeking a more effective, scalable way to generate leads and grow their business.

- **Any life insurance professional** looking to embrace the power of digital marketing to achieve six-figure success faster than ever before.

Let's Begin

The journey to six-figure success is challenging but entirely within reach. By the end of this book, you'll have the insights, tools, and confidence to thrive as a life insurance agent in today's digital landscape. Whether you're a newcomer or a seasoned pro, this roadmap is your blueprint for success.

So, are you ready to leave outdated techniques behind and unlock the potential of digital marketing? If so, let's dive in.

SIX FIGURES IN 12 MONTHS

CHAPTER 1

The Foundation of Success

Small Thinking, Small Results

When I first joined the life insurance business, I was a small thinker. Not because I lacked ambition, but because I had limited exposure to what was possible. The people around me—the ones who had introduced me to the industry—weren't exactly crushing it. Most were scraping by, making just enough to survive. Naturally, my goals reflected that. My initial aim was to make $5,000 in three months.

At the time, that felt monumental. No one in my circle was earning that kind of money in such a short time. For me, hitting $5,000 was more than just financial—it was validation. It was proof that I could succeed in an industry that many doubted. But in truth, my thinking was limited to the capacity of the people around me. I thought small because the people around me were thinking small and as a result achieved small results.

"You are the average of the five people you spend the most time with." — Jim Rohn

They weren't bad people, nor did they lack potential. But their vision of success was narrow, and I adopted it as my own. I convinced myself that $5,000 in three months was the limit because that's all I saw. Then, I encountered someone doing far more—someone who shattered that limit entirely.

The Turning Point: When My Mindset Changed

One day, seeking inspiration, I stumbled across a podcast that would forever alter my career trajectory. The guest was a young life insurance agent, under 30, talking about his career. When he casually mentioned earning an average of $40,000 per month, I couldn't believe it. In a business where many struggled to make ends meet, here was someone earning $40,000—*a month.*

I was stunned. This was no magic trick; he wasn't doing anything supernatural. He was simply disciplined, consistent, and believed in his potential. That podcast didn't just give me a new target; it changed my entire mindset. If someone else could make $40,000 a month in the same industry, why couldn't I?

The Power of Belief

That podcast was my *Roger Bannister moment.* For those who don't know, Roger Bannister was the first person to run a mile in under four minutes. Before he accomplished this feat in 1954, no one thought it was possible. But once he broke that barrier, it became real for everyone else. Today, over 1,700 people have run a sub-four-minute mile. Bannister didn't show others their physical capability—he unlocked the power of belief.

> "All things are possible to those who believe." — Mark 9:23

Just like Bannister, that young agent on the podcast expanded my belief system and gave me the courage to dream bigger. I realized belief isn't just a motivator; it's the foundation of everything you achieve. Once you truly believe in your goal, your mind works in ways to make it happen. This was the beginning of my commitment to earning $20,000 a month and beyond.

Programming Your Mind for Success with Daily Affirmations

When I committed to earning $20,000 a month, I knew it wasn't enough to want it—I had to believe it. This is when I began reprogramming my mind through daily affirmations. Affirmations are short, positive statements that reinforce the beliefs you want to cultivate. They shape your mindset over time, leading to real behavioral changes.

Some affirmations I used included:

- *"I am now earning $20,000-a-month in my life insurance business."*
- *"Money comes to me easily and effortlessly."*
- *"I am a money magnet."*

At first, it felt odd. A part of me thought, "Who am I to say this when I'm nowhere near that goal?" But that's the magic of affirmations—they don't reflect your *current* reality; they shape your *future* reality. As I repeated these affirmations, they started sinking into my subconscious mind, creating a powerful transformation.

How the Subconscious Mind Works

Your subconscious mind is the driving force behind your actions and beliefs. While your conscious mind handles daily thoughts, your subconscious operates below the surface, guiding your habits, reactions, and deeply held beliefs.

"Whatever we plant in our subconscious mind and nourish with repetition and emotion will one day become a reality." — Earl Nightingale

The subconscious mind doesn't distinguish between reality and imagination—it accepts what you tell it. That's why affirmations are so powerful. When you repeat positive statements, your subconscious mind believes them. Eventually, these beliefs embed in your subconscious, and your behavior naturally aligns with them.

When I started affirming I was a $20,000-a-month earner, my subconscious accepted it as truth. Once that belief took hold, my actions followed suit. I worked differently, thought differently, and showed up differently. That's the magic of the subconscious—it shapes your reality based on what you believe.

From $20,000 to $50,000: The Power of Belief Expansion

Reaching my $20,000 goal was transformative, but it also taught me that if I could reach one milestone, why not aim higher? I set a new target of $50,000, using the same belief-centered approach. As Brian Tracy explains, our external results always reflect our internal beliefs. Small thinking leads to small results, but big thinking leads to extraordinary achievements.

"Your life is a reflection of your thoughts. Change your thinking, and you change your life." — Brian Tracy

The Role of Discipline and Daily Action

Belief is essential, but belief alone isn't enough. The young man in the podcast wasn't earning $40,000 a month by accident. He had a system—a daily routine to support his big goals.

I modeled my actions on his. I created a daily routine aligned with my goals. Every morning, I reminded myself of what I was working toward, and every day, I took steps toward it. Whether I was improving my product knowledge, reaching new prospects, or creating content, I ensured my actions aligned with my beliefs.

"Success is the sum of small efforts, repeated day in and day out." — Robert Collier

Believe First, Then Watch What Happens

If there's one lesson I want you to take from this chapter, it's that belief is the foundation of success. No strategy, no tool, no amount of effort will work unless you first believe you can achieve your goals. Once you hold that belief, everything else follows.

Unlocking Your Potential Through Belief

My journey from a small-thinking agent with a $5,000 goal to an ambitious entrepreneur aiming for $50,000 a month didn't happen overnight. It started with a shift in mindset—a belief that something bigger was possible. That belief led me to take bold actions, embrace new opportunities, and build a thriving career.

The same is possible for you. It doesn't matter where you're starting from; what matters is where you believe you can go. As you continue reading, remember that your belief will be the catalyst for everything else. The strategies in this book will only work if you first believe they're possible.

"Miracles happen when you believe."

Reflection Exercise: Unlocking Your Potential Through Belief

To embed the lessons from this chapter into your own life, complete these exercises:

1. **Identify Your Influences**: Who are the five people you spend the most time with? Reflect on how their beliefs impact yours and whether they inspire or limit you.

2. **Expand Your Vision**: Write down a financial goal you currently have. Is it big enough, or is it limited by what you think is achievable? Rewrite that goal without limits.

3. **Practice Affirmations**: Choose an affirmation that resonates with you or create your own. Repeat it daily for 30 days and journal any changes in your mindset.

SIX FIGURES IN 12 MONTHS

CHAPTER 2

Master the Basics of Life Insurance: Carve Out Your Expertise

The Insurance Ecosystem

The life insurance industry is a diverse and expansive ecosystem, with products tailored to meet the needs of clients at every stage of life. From term life insurance to whole life, indexed universal life (IUL) policies, and final expense insurance, each product has unique benefits and limitations. Thriving in this industry isn't about selling everything to everyone; it's about specializing, becoming an expert, and building trust. This focused approach not only sets you apart but also builds credibility with clients who are seeking clarity in an often confusing market.

"An investment in knowledge pays the best interest." — Benjamin Franklin

High-performing agents aren't generalists; they're specialists. By focusing on one product, they master it, build trust, and become the go-to expert for that solution. This focus allows clients to feel understood, making them more likely to refer others and become loyal customers.

My Journey to Expertise

In my early days, I realized that life insurance sales were less about aggressive persuasion and more about client education. But initially, my own knowledge was too shallow to provide the guidance clients needed. I knew the basics, yet lacked the deeper understanding required to explain complex products clearly and confidently. This was particularly challenging with a complex product like IUL, which offers unique wealth-building potential but can seem daunting without sufficient knowledge.

Unfortunately, the team I initially joined didn't prioritize this type of in-depth learning. I found myself struggling to communicate IUL's benefits effectively, and clients sensed my lack of confidence. Quickly, I understood that if I wanted to succeed, I had to go beyond my team's limited resources. I reached out to the insurance carrier's sales department, scheduled training sessions, and engaged in intense three-day sessions where they broke down the inner workings of IUL.

These sessions unlocked a deeper understanding that fundamentally changed my approach. I complemented this learning with independent study—reading books, watching expert-led videos, and networking with top performers in the industry. The more I learned, the more confident I became in my ability to explain complex products in simple, relatable terms. This shift allowed me to educate my clients more effectively and, in turn, increased my sales significantly.

"The more you learn, the more you earn."

By building content around IUL and educating my audience, I was able to turn this complex product into something approachable and attractive for clients. Prospective clients started coming to me not because I was the loudest or most visible agent but because I had valuable knowledge to share. This transformation highlighted the power of being a true expert in your field

Specializing in a Niche: The Path to Industry Leadership

Here's a crucial lesson I learned: thriving in life insurance requires specialization. While it might feel like casting a wide net is the fastest way to gain business, the opposite is true. Choosing a specific product niche, mastering it, and focusing your energy there makes you stand out, attracting the right clients. For me, that specialization was IUL, and this focus allowed me to dominate a market that many agents overlooked or only touched on briefly.

When clients think of insurance, they don't want a "one-size-fits-all" solution—they want guidance from someone who genuinely understands their chosen product. By committing to one product, whether it's IUL, term life, or whole life, you become known for that expertise, and clients seek you out for your unique insights.

"If you want to be successful, you must become an expert in your field. People do business with experts, not generalists." — John C. Maxwell

By specializing, you position yourself as a resource that clients can depend on, especially as they seek tailored solutions for their financial goals. Clients feel more comfortable and confident working with a specialist rather than someone who tries to sell every available product.

Educating the Market: Building Trust and Credibility

Education is one of the most powerful tools an agent can leverage in this industry. I learned that clients want life insurance, but often don't understand how it can serve their financial goals. By taking the time to educate, you become more than a salesperson; you become a trusted advisor. For example, I made it my mission to simplify complex concepts around IUL, showing clients how they could use it as a vehicle to grow wealth, borrow tax-free, and plan for a secure future. This level of clarity helped clients see life insurance as an empowering tool rather than just a monthly expense.

As I shared valuable insights on social media and during consultations, clients grew more interested in purchasing IUL policies because they understood the product's real benefits. This approach not only led to steady business growth but also attracted clients who were genuinely interested in building financial stability. Remarkably, I achieved this without paying for ads or leads; clients were drawn to me because I offered expertise and guidance they couldn't easily find elsewhere.

Understanding the Insurance Ecosystem: A Quick Overview

To gain a comprehensive understanding of life insurance products, here's a breakdown of major offerings and their ideal clients:

Product	Ideal Clients	Key Benefits
Term Life Insurance	Young families, short-term needs	Affordability and simplicity, ideal for temporary coverage
Whole Life Insurance	Lifelong coverage seekers	Guaranteed death benefit and cash value that grows over time
Indexed Universal Life	Wealth builders, tax-advantaged growth	Cash value growth linked to market performance with downside protection
Variable Universal Life	Investment-focused clients	Market-based cash value growth with potential for higher returns
Final Expense Insurance	Seniors, limited budgets	Affordable, no medical exams, covers end-of-life expenses

Carving Out Your Niche: Building Your Own Ark

Finding a niche in this ecosystem is akin to building an "ark" in a sea of generalists. While others are selling a mix of term, whole life, and final expense policies, your expertise in a specific product will set you apart.

"The man who chases two rabbits catches neither." — Confucius

Defining Your Niche: Key Questions

Here are some questions to help you identify the right niche:

1. **What product resonates with me?** Choose a product that aligns with your strengths and interests, as passion is key to client engagement.

2. **How knowledgeable am I?** Commit to becoming a subject matter expert in your chosen product. Knowledge is the foundation of confidence and success.

3. **Who are my ideal clients?** Identify the clients who would benefit most from your product, and tailor your approach to their needs and challenges.

4. **Where do my clients spend time?** Find out where your clients gather—online or offline—and meet them there.

5. **What skills do I need to develop?** Develop any skills that will help you effectively reach and serve your ideal clients, such as social media, public speaking, or financial planning.

6. **Who do I need to become to attract my ideal clients?** Success is a journey of personal growth. Strive to become a knowledgeable, approachable expert who inspires trust.

Quote for Reflection:
"The big man with the big problem is easier to sell than the small man with the small problem." — Ben Feldman

The Expert Advantage

Specialization not only builds your expertise but also establishes trust with clients, resulting in greater loyalty, more referrals, and a sustainable business model.

Building a niche-focused business may feel limiting at first, but it actually opens the door to long-term success, increased revenue, and stronger client relationships. Specializing in a specific product transforms you into the expert clients are seeking, allowing you to stand out in a crowded market.

SIX FIGURES IN 12 MONTHS

CHAPTER 3

The Money Is In the Niches

How I Carved Out My Own Niche

When I first started in life insurance, I was eager and full of ideas but lacked direction. I spent each day creating content on diverse topics, from family insurance benefits to IUL perks for young professionals. This wide net approach gave me some success but didn't lead to deep client engagement. My messaging was scattered, and I found it hard to build a dedicated client base. Without a focused niche, I was essentially competing with every other agent in the market.

Realizing that I needed a specific target, I made a key decision: I focused exclusively on entrepreneurs and high-income earners. Being an entrepreneur myself, I could relate to their unique financial goals and challenges. This shift allowed me to speak their language, connect authentically, and deliver solutions that felt personalized.

"Think small, and your cases will be small. Think big, and your cases will be big." — Ben Feldman

Focusing on this niche transformed my results. Instead of convincing everyone to buy a policy, I was helping a particular audience see how my solutions fit their needs. With this clarity, my strategy sharpened, and I began securing larger policies, ultimately leading to higher income. Today, roughly 80% of my clients are entrepreneurs and high-income earners, allowing me to stand out and build a specialized reputation in the industry.

Why Many Agents Struggle

Many agents come into life insurance believing that casting a wide net will increase their chances of success. This "sell to everyone" mindset places them in direct competition with other agents, saturating the market with generic messages and solutions.

Ben Feldman, a highly successful agent, once said, "If you want big volume, you have to look for prospects with big price tags on their problems." He focused on high-value clients with complex needs, and his approach didn't involve appealing to everyone. Instead, he specialized in serving clients with high-value solutions and tailored strategies.

The most successful agents do the opposite of the majority: they carve out a niche, concentrate on a specific audience, and build trust and expertise within that area. Instead of diluting their energy across various products and client types, they commit to serving a well-defined group.

Carving Your Own Niche: Why It's Essential

Success in life insurance is not about reaching the widest audience but rather finding a well-defined market and serving it with excellence. Here's why focusing on a niche is crucial:

1. **Reduced Competition**: Specializing removes you from the pool of general agents competing for everyone's business. You position yourself as the expert for a specific group, automatically reducing competition and increasing your appeal.

2. **Clear, Powerful Messaging**: A focused audience allows you to craft messaging that resonates deeply. By addressing the unique needs of your niche, you create stronger connections and build trust.

3. **Higher-Quality Clients**: Working in a niche attracts clients who value what you offer and are financially prepared, aligned with your services, and more likely to become long-term clients.

4. **Greater Success with Less Effort**: Real success comes from quality, not quantity. As the book *10X Is Easier Than 2X* points out, "Working too many hours means you're living 2X, not 10X." Real success involves a clear focus on high-impact efforts.

5. **Scalability**: A defined niche allows you to create systems and content that consistently serve a specific

audience, enabling you to grow without stretching yourself too thin.

Examples of Niche Markets for Insurance Products

Consider these examples of how different life insurance products serve niche audiences:

- **Truck Drivers and IUL**: Self-employed truck drivers lack employer retirement plans. IUL offers them life insurance and wealth-building options, with tax-advantaged growth.

- **Medical Professionals and IUL**: Nurses and medical professionals often lack time for investment management. IUL provides a stable, long-term financial tool with tax-free growth and limited management.

- **Single Moms and Term Life**: Term life policies offer single mothers affordable financial protection, addressing a specific need for security without overwhelming cost.

- **Real Estate Investors and Term Life for Mortgage Protection**: Real estate investors often carry large mortgages. Term life insurance can cover these debts, offering peace of mind for clients with significant assets.

By identifying a niche and creating content specifically tailored to its needs, you become the go-to expert, building credibility, trust, and a steady flow of ideal clients.

Blue Ocean Strategy: Creating Your Own Market

The *Blue Ocean Strategy* offers a powerful framework for niche marketing. Instead of competing in the "red ocean" of intense competition, agents can create a "blue ocean"—an uncontested market space by serving an underserved group. Here's how you can apply this strategy:

1. **Eliminate**: Remove complex jargon and simplify messaging to make your products accessible.

2. **Reduce**: Focus on fewer but highly relevant product features.

3. **Raise**: Emphasize aspects that matter most to your audience, like tax-free growth for business owners.

4. **Create**: Add unique value, such as specialized educational content or personalized guidance.

For instance, in targeting entrepreneurs with IUL, you could eliminate unnecessary jargon, focus on the benefits of tax-free growth, and create unique content addressing the financial goals of business owners.

"Going for 10X requires letting go of 80% of your current life and focus and going all-in on the crucial 20 percent that's relevant and high impact." — *10X Is Easier Than 2X*

Niche Success Stories: Companies That Thrived

Companies like Apple and Tesla are powerful examples of niche focus. Apple caters to design-driven, high-end consumers, while Tesla serves environmentally conscious drivers. Both companies dominate their industries because they prioritized niche appeal over broad market reach.

Focus on One Niche and Be the Best at Meeting Their Needs

Life insurance rewards specialization. Instead of casting a wide net, find your niche, tailor your approach to its needs, and commit to being the best. This focus will increase your revenue, foster strong client relationships, and create a sustainable, profitable business.

"You can't be everything to everyone, but you can be everything to someone."

CHAPTER 4

Strategies to Dominate on Social Media

How I Went from Unknown Agent to Recognized Expert

Earlier on in my career as a life insurance agent, I was determined to be successful and make it work. I started by trying to drum up business through family and friends, which is often the most common method taught to new agents. I was told to write down the names of everyone I knew—friends, family, old colleagues—and use a scripted approach to introduce them to life insurance or the industry itself. It's supposed to be an easy way to get started without spending money on advertising. But the reality was different.

Within weeks, I was feeling the strain of this strategy, especially when my calls started getting ignored. I began to see the flaws in relying solely on friends and family to build my business. Not everyone is interested in life insurance, and trying to convince them wasn't just exhausting—it was a quick path to burnout.

One moment, in particular, stands out. About two weeks after getting my license, a close friend mentioned he was interested in starting his own insurance agency. Since I was already involved in the industry, I decided to introduce him to the organization I had partnered with. I set up a Zoom call with a senior marketing director, expecting a simple 15-minute chat. Instead, the meeting turned into a nearly two-hour pitch filled with confusing details and vague promises. My friend was left feeling overwhelmed and skeptical, and he stopped answering my calls after that. That experience was a turning point for me. I decided then and there that I would never rely on friends and family to build my success in this industry.

This shift in thinking is what led me to social media.

Today, social media is my main client pipeline. With a following that has grown to over **700,000 across various platforms** (TikTok, Instagram, Facebook, and YouTube), I have turned social media into a powerful tool that connects me with people who genuinely want to learn about life insurance and wealth-building. By creating content that resonates, informs, and answers common questions, I have moved from a place of pursuing leads to having leads find me.

The Crucial Role of Social Media in the 21st Century

In today's digital-first world, social media isn't just a brand awareness tool—it's a powerful business driver. With over 4.9 billion active users globally, each platform offers unique engagement opportunities. For life insurance agents, understanding and leveraging these platforms is essential to staying competitive and relevant. Here's why mastering social media matters:

1. **Broad Reach and Targeted Audiences**: Social media makes life insurance accessible to a vast, diverse audience while allowing for targeted demographic advertising. For example, Facebook is effective for reaching an older demographic familiar with traditional insurance needs, while TikTok and Instagram cater to younger audiences eager to learn about innovative financial products like Indexed Universal Life (IUL).

2. **Affordability**: Social media provides low-cost or free options to reach thousands, if not millions, of potential clients. By dedicating time to consistent posting and engagement, you can achieve a significant return on investment without a large upfront cost.

3. **Educational Potential**: Agents can create informative content explaining life insurance benefits, policy types, and wealth-building strategies. Education builds trust and creates more organic, value-driven sales.

4. **Real-Time Interaction and Relationship Building**: Social media allows for instant interaction, helping you engage with clients in real time, answer questions, and build rapport faster than other methods.

5. **Data-Driven Marketing**: Analytics tools on platforms like Facebook, Instagram, and TikTok help you understand who's engaging with your content and how, providing data to refine your approach.

6. **Authority Building**: Consistent, valuable content fosters brand recognition. As you build familiarity, clients are more likely to choose you over competitors in a highly personal field like life insurance.

How Social Media Transformed My Business

Moving from direct outreach to social media was a breakthrough. In December 2021, when posted my first TikTok video on life insurance, I had no clue that that one content would change my life forever. To my surprise, it quickly amassed over 40,000 views. Within days, hundreds of thousands of people were engaging with my content. The best part? People I'd never met were reaching out, ready to learn more. As I continued to post more content flood of leads were coming in daily. I was helping two to four clients get set up with IUL every day, a product they now saw as a valuable financial tool.

This experience redefined my approach. By sharing educational content that tackled topics like IUL benefits and debunking life insurance myths, I created a steady flow of leads. Within months, I went from 27 followers on TikTok to hundreds of thousands across platforms, growing my client base and elevating my business.

Becoming a Producer Instead of a Consumer

One of the fundamental changes I made early on was shifting from a consumer mindset to a producer mindset. Here's what that means in practical terms:

- **Consumers**: They scroll through content, like posts, and passively absorb information. Many agents fall into this trap, spending hours watching what others are doing without contributing to the space.

- **Producers**: They create, share, and consistently publish valuable content that educates, entertains, or inspires their target audience. Producers are active participants in the platform's ecosystem, and they're the ones who build authority and attract followers.

By switching to a producer mindset, I became intentional about my social media activity. Each post had a purpose—whether it was to educate, answer a common question, or build credibility. Being a producer means that every time you log on, you're contributing, not just consuming. It's this active role that leads to greater visibility and growth.

Getting Started: Social Media Strategies for New Agents

If you're new to social media, it can be overwhelming. Here's how to start building an online presence effectively:

1. **Start with Consistency**: Pick one or two platforms to begin with and commit to a consistent posting

schedule. Even one post per week is enough to start building trust.

2. **Educational Content as Your Foundation**: Share posts that add value, such as videos on life insurance benefits, infographics about policy types, and answers to common questions. Consistent, educational content fosters trust and authority.

3. **Master the Art of Storytelling**; Share personal and client success stories to humanize your content. When people see real-life benefits, they're more likely to connect with you.

4. **Keep Production Simple**: You don't need an expensive studio setup. A smartphone, ring light, and editing apps like Capcut, Caption or Canva are enough to create engaging content that looks professional.

5. **Engage with Your Audience**: Take time to respond to comments and direct messages. Building a community means making your followers feel valued and seen.

6. **Analyze and Adjust**: Use analytics to track what content resonates. Refine your strategy based on real data to improve engagement over time.

The Importance of Visibility: Attention Drives Success

In an industry as competitive as life insurance, visibility is critical. Your expertise and services are valuable, but if no one knows about them, they don't exist in the minds of potential clients. Visibility on social media builds awareness and establishes you as a trustworthy figure in the industry.

Here's why attention is crucial:

1. **Building Credibility and Trust**: When people see you regularly sharing valuable information, you become a trusted source. They begin to view you as a subject matter expert, which builds credibility—a key component in an industry where trust is essential.

2. **Creating Familiarity**: The "familiarity effect" means that the more someone sees you, the more likely they are to trust and feel comfortable reaching out. Frequent content helps your audience feel like they know you, even before a direct conversation.

3. **Establishing Authority**: Life insurance isn't new, but your unique perspective and voice are. When you're visible, sharing your insights, people recognize your authority and are more likely to choose you over others.

4. **Increasing Organic Reach**: On social media, algorithms reward consistency and engagement. The more visible you are, the higher the likelihood that your content will reach a larger audience organically, expanding your reach without additional advertising spend.

5. **Being "Top of Mind" for Your Audience**: When people see your posts regularly, you're at the forefront of their minds when they think about life insurance. If they—or someone they know—need a policy, you'll be the one they remember.

Five Secrets to Winning with Social Media

1. **Have an Active Presence**: Don't just exist on the platform—actively post, engage, and create valuable content that connects with your audience.

2. **Choose the Right Platforms**: Tailor your content to platform strengths:
    - TikTok: Short, viral videos
    - Instagram: Stories, reels, educational posts
    - Facebook: Group engagement, longer posts
    - YouTube: In-depth videos, tutorials

3. **Prioritize Educational Content**: Consistently educate your audience. Topics could include explaining different life insurance options, tax benefits of IULs, or how insurance fits into wealth-building strategies.

4. **Focus on Quality Engagement**: Focus on creating meaningful connections with your followers. Build relationships that extend beyond just selling a product.

5. **Be Patient and Persistent**: Social media success isn't instant. It requires patience, consistency, and a

commitment to showing up, even when results aren't immediate.

Creating a Client-Generating Powerhouse

By remaining visible, consistent, and dedicated to providing value, you can turn social media into a powerful client-generating tool. In the next chapters, we'll explore advanced strategies for scaling and systemizing your business, helping you leverage visibility into a sustainable, profitable practice.

SIX FIGURES IN 12 MONTHS

CHAPTER 5

Attraction Marketing: Creating Engaging Content That Sells

Building Your Brand Through Attraction Marketing

In today's digital landscape, attraction marketing is a powerful strategy. It's about drawing people to you by consistently delivering valuable content without pushing for a sale. When potential clients see you sharing insights, explaining key concepts, and answering their questions, they're naturally inclined to reach out. With over 700,000 followers across platforms, my experience has shown that consistently delivering quality, attraction-focused content not only educates your audience but also builds lasting connections that convert followers into loyal clients.

What Makes Videos Go Viral?

Creating viral content isn't about luck; it's about a formula that captures attention and encourages sharing. Here's what I've found makes a video resonate:

1. **A Strong Hook**: The hook is everything. The first few seconds determine whether people keep watching or scroll past. An effective hook can be a provocative question, a surprising fact, or a relatable statement that immediately engages your viewer. Without a strong opening, even the best content can go unseen.

2. **Emotion and Relatability**: Videos that strike an emotional chord are shared more frequently. Whether it's humor, empathy, or inspiration, tapping into emotions makes your content memorable.

3. **Concise, Clear Message**: Simplicity is crucial. A viral video should deliver a message that's easy to understand and remember. Aim to keep videos concise—90 seconds or less for platforms like Instagram Reels and TikTok.

4. **Clear Call-to-Action (CTA)**: Give viewers a reason to engage, like asking them to comment, share, or tag a friend. Higher engagement signals to the platform that your content is valuable, which increases its visibility.

5. **Use of Trending Elements**: Leveraging popular sounds, music, or hashtags can increase your reach. When your video aligns with trends, it's more likely to appear on explore pages and reach new viewers.

By focusing on these elements, I've created videos that have reached millions of viewers, grown my follower base, and generated genuine leads. The good news is that you can do the same thing.

Strategies for Creating Compelling Content That Attracts Ideal Clients

Creating content that attracts your ideal clients starts with understanding their needs and interests. Here's how to build engagement:

1. **Educational Tips and Explainers**: Educational content that breaks down financial terms like "term life insurance" resonates well. For instance, I often use a whiteboard to illustrate key points visually, which makes concepts more accessible. Visual aids help simplify complex information, making it easier for people to grasp.

2. **Real-Life Examples and Stories**: Stories and real-life examples make your content relatable. If you're explaining term life insurance, consider illustrating the concept by comparing it to rental versus ownership. Visuals allow viewers to see the benefits and limitations of term life policies more clearly.

3. **Behind-the-Scenes Insights**: Authenticity builds trust. Sharing a glimpse into your day or offering personal insights into why you do what you do makes your audience feel more connected.

4. **Interactive Content**: Quizzes, polls, and Q&A sessions invite followers to interact. These formats allow your audience to engage with you directly, building familiarity and trust.

The Power of Duets: How Juan Franco Found Success with This Strategy

One of the most effective ways to gain traction on social media is by using the duet feature, especially on TikTok. Duets allow you to split your screen with someone else's video, adding your reactions or insights. This feature can drive huge engagement, introducing you to a wider audience. Juan Franco, a seasoned life insurance agent, provides an excellent example of how powerful duets can be. In his early sixties, Juan was struggling with the traditional methods of door-knocking and face-to-face client meetings. Then he discovered social media and came across one of my videos explaining the power of life insurance. He duetted my video, pointing at the screen with his facial expression. The duet reached over 1 million views—more than the original video—and generated a flood of leads for Juan.

Recognizing the potential of duets, he started regularly engaging with popular financial videos, sharing his own insights, and building credibility. Over time, Juan grew his following to nearly 600,000 across TikTok, Instagram, and Facebook. His strategy evolved into a powerful social media presence that transformed his business into over $1million in less than 12 months. So it's safe to say that the strategy works.

Repurposing Content from Other Industries

Content ideas don't always have to be original—some of the most effective content can come from adapting popular concepts in unrelated fields. Here are some examples of how to repurpose successful ideas from other industries for the financial field:

1. **"Behind-the-Scenes" Inspired by Chefs**: Chefs often post videos of their cooking process, creating a "behind-the-scenes" feel. You can adapt this by sharing a behind-the-scenes look at your day as a financial professional, like preparing for a client meeting or conducting research.

2. **"Myth-Busting" Inspired by Fitness Influencers**: Fitness experts often debunk common workout myths, which drives engagement. In the financial industry, consider creating "myths about life insurance" videos to address common misconceptions.

3. **"Day in the Life" Inspired by Lifestyle Influencers**: Many lifestyle influencers post "day in the life" content. A "day in the life of a financial expert" video can help humanize you, making you more relatable and trustworthy.

Repurposing popular content from other industries not only saves time but also helps you engage with your audience in a familiar, approachable way.

Batch Content Creation: My Story of Consistency

One of the most challenging yet crucial aspects of growing on social media is consistency. Early on, I made it a practice to batch-create content. This meant I'd spend an entire day at my office with 5-7 outfits and create multiple videos in one sitting. With each outfit, I'd film around three videos, resulting in 15-21 pieces of content in one day.

Creating each video took planning. I wrote scripts carefully, often using a teleprompter app to keep my message clear and concise. Each script was under 90 seconds to fit Instagram Reel limits, which required researching and thinking about the most direct way to deliver value. This process took around 2-3 hours, and once I was done filming, I'd spend several hours editing. Throughout the week, I'd post three videos daily—morning, afternoon, and evening—ensuring consistent visibility.

Today, AI tools make this process easier. AI can generate multiple scripts per day, allowing you to focus on tweaking and refining rather than starting from scratch. This saves time and lets you concentrate on content quality and strategy.

Establishing a Posting Schedule

Consistency doesn't end with content creation; having a strategic posting schedule is essential. I post at three specific times—morning, afternoon, and evening—to reach followers throughout the day. This way, I stay top-of-mind and maximize engagement by meeting people during different parts of their routine. Developing a schedule also helps your audience know when to expect your content, increasing the likelihood of views.

Engaging with Followers to Build Relationships

Building a loyal audience requires more than just posting. I make it a point to consistently respond to comments and messages. By engaging with followers, I show them that they're more than just numbers; they're valued members of my community. Responding to comments makes followers feel seen and appreciated, which strengthens their connection to you and makes them more likely to support your content and, ultimately, your business.

The Power of a Strong Hook in Impacting Views

An effective hook is the difference between someone watching your entire video or scrolling past. A good hook should immediately grab attention, pique curiosity, or address a relatable issue. The hook doesn't have to be complicated; sometimes, a simple, powerful statement like, "Why the poor and middle class don't buy life insurance" can pull viewers in. Mastering the hook will dramatically improve your content's visibility and engagement.

Attraction Marketing in Action

Attraction marketing is about drawing clients to you through engaging, consistent, and valuable content. By incorporating a strong hook, strategic engagement, consistent posting, and

SIX FIGURES IN 12 MONTHS

leveraging batch creation, you establish a powerful social media presence that builds credibility and trust.

Remember, creating engaging content doesn't have to be overwhelming. Use these strategies to make the most of every piece of content, consistently draw people in, and turn followers into clients.

CHAPTER 6

Build a Magnetic Personal Brand

The Power of Brand: The Story of Nike's Rise

The story of Nike is one of the most powerful examples of how branding can turn a company into an icon. In the 1960s and '70s, Nike was just another name in a crowded athletic market. Phil Knight and Bill Bowerman, Nike's founders, understood that selling shoes alone would not be enough to compete with giants like Adidas and Puma. They needed a brand that resonated with a universal message. So, in 1988, Nike launched the legendary "Just Do It" campaign—a slogan that embodied ambition, determination, and resilience. It wasn't about selling shoes; it was about inspiring people to push past their limits and believe in their potential.

Nike's brand message grew far beyond its products. It became a lifestyle and a call to action that attracted athletes and non-athletes alike. By tapping into the emotions of people striving to overcome challenges, Nike positioned itself as a brand that wasn't just about sports; it was about self-belief and pushing past limitations. Today, the Nike swoosh represents much more than athletic gear; it stands for the spirit of perseverance, success, and ambition. This transformation was made possible by the consistency of Nike's messaging, the strength of its values, and its ability to create an emotional bond with customers.

How Nike's Story Applies to Building a Financial Brand

Nike's story shows that a strong brand identity goes beyond selling products. It's about creating a connection based on shared values and aspirations. In financial services, your brand can also transcend products like life insurance or wealth-building strategies. Instead, your brand can be built around helping clients achieve financial freedom, security, and peace of mind. Like Nike, you're not just selling a service; you're providing clients with a pathway to a more secure and empowered future.

My Journey to Building a Personal Brand as a Financial Expert

When I started in financial services, I knew I wanted to stand out for more than just life insurance sales. My goal was to become a trusted financial expert, known for providing valuable, actionable insights on wealth-building, financial literacy, and financial well-being. I saw many agents limit themselves to just selling insurance, but I wanted to build a brand that spoke to the broader picture of financial health.

To achieve this, I began sharing insights on everything from debt management to building generational wealth. Instead of limiting my focus to life insurance, I positioned it as one piece of a larger financial strategy. This broader approach not only distinguished me from others in the industry but also attracted clients who were committed to long-term financial success. By providing valuable information, I created a brand that felt more like a resource than a sales pitch, and clients began seeking me out as a trusted advisor.

Authenticity as the Foundation of Your Brand

Authenticity is the cornerstone of a powerful personal brand, especially in an era when audiences are highly attuned to genuine voices. Building a personal brand starts with understanding who you are, what you bring to the table, and how you can best serve others. Rather than trying to copy what's working for others, focus on what makes you unique—your experiences, insights, and values.

In her book *Influencer*, Brittany Hennessy notes that today's audiences crave transparency and authenticity. Consumers are increasingly drawn to brands that share their values and are willing to go beyond sales to build real connections. For financial professionals, this means building a brand around helping clients achieve their dreams, creating stability for their families, or pursuing long-term goals. By aligning your brand with values that resonate with your audience, you create trust and loyalty.

Example Application: If you're passionate about fitness, consider creating a brand that bridges financial health with physical wellness. You could share insights into how financial security enhances well-being, naturally incorporating financial services into your content. This blend of interests can help you stand out and connect deeply with a specific audience.

Tips from Hennessy's Approach:

1. **Know Your Audience**: Define who your ideal clients are and what motivates them. Tailor your messaging to address their unique goals.

2. **Be Transparent**: Share your story and your "why." Authenticity builds loyalty and establishes a deeper connection with clients.

3. **Provide Real Value**: Offer actionable advice that empowers clients, enhancing your brand's value beyond financial products.

Reflection: *"People can tell when you're only selling them something. True influence comes from genuine connection."*
— Brittany Hennessy

Crafting a Distinct Identity

To stand out, you need to answer three fundamental questions: Who are you? What do you stand for? And why should clients choose you? Michael Johnson, in his book *Branding*, emphasizes that a compelling brand story is rooted in these answers. When you can clearly articulate your mission, your values, and your unique approach, you build a brand identity that resonates deeply.

Example Application: If you have experience in real estate, you could position yourself as an expert in real estate-backed financial planning, providing tips on property investment and strategies for securing real estate assets. This combination allows you to stand out and attract clients with similar interests.

Practical Applications from Johnson's Work:

1. **Define Your Core Message**: Decide what you want to be known for, whether it's wealth-building for entrepreneurs, financial literacy for young professionals, or legacy planning for families.

2. **Create a Visual Identity**: Use consistent colors, fonts, and imagery to make your brand easily recognizable.

3. **Share Your Story**: Share your journey and why you're passionate about financial services. Stories connect people and build brand loyalty.

Reflection: "People remember stories, not statistics. Tell your story well, and they'll remember you." — Michael Johnson

Adding Value to Build Trust

In *This is Marketing*, Seth Godin explains that people don't just want a product; they want to know why it's being offered and how it will improve their lives. This insight is essential in financial services, where trust is everything. Your goal is to educate clients, empower them, and show them the value of financial products like life insurance as part of a larger financial plan.

Example Application: If you're passionate about youth financial literacy, build a brand that educates young adults on the fundamentals—budgeting, saving, and debt management. As they learn to navigate these basics, life insurance can be introduced as a key component in long-term planning, making you a trusted educator and advisor.

Examples of Unique Brand Building Approaches

Creating a brand doesn't mean you have to focus solely on life insurance or financial services. Here are some ways to blend your interests with financial services to create a unique, compelling brand:

1. **Fitness and Financial Health**: Establish yourself as a wellness advocate, combining physical and financial wellness tips. Show how financial stability can enhance overall health, with life insurance as a piece of a balanced life plan.

2. **Entrepreneurial Finance**: Target small business owners by sharing wealth-building tips and income protection plans, incorporating life insurance as a tool for securing business assets.

3. **Real Estate and Financial Security**: Combine property investment insights with financial strategies, positioning life insurance as a way to protect real estate investments.

4. **Travel and Financial Independence**: Create content around achieving financial independence to support a life of travel and adventure.

5. **Parenting and Family Finances**: Offer financial advice geared towards families, including topics like saving for college and creating a legacy.

6. **Career Development and Financial Planning**: Share strategies for young professionals to manage income wisely, positioning life insurance as a foundation for long-term security.

Reflection: *"A brand is a story that is always being told."*
— Scott Bedbury

The Benefits of a Strong Personal Brand in Financial Services

Building a strong personal brand has fueled substantial growth in my business. Here's how a well-defined brand can elevate your success:

- **Attract High-Quality Clients**: Clients are drawn to trusted experts with a clear identity.

- **Build Lasting Relationships**: A strong brand encourages loyalty and repeat business.

- **Stand Out in a Crowded Market**: A unique identity differentiates you from other agents.

- **Expand Your Influence**: Increased brand recognition leads to greater impact and opportunity.

Build a Brand That Lasts

Building a brand is a commitment, but the rewards are transformative. With consistency, a clear mission, and a deep understanding of your clients' needs, your brand can become a trusted resource, attracting loyal clients and creating lasting impact.

Reflection: *"Your brand is what people say about you when you're not in the room."* — Jeff Bezos

Building a personal brand isn't only about promoting financial products. By sharing your insights, telling your story, and genuinely helping others achieve financial goals, you create a brand that resonates, builds trust, and makes a meaningful difference in clients' lives.

CHAPTER 7

Increase Sales by 10X: Setting Up Automation and Systems

The Power of Systems—Lessons from McDonald's Journey to Global Success

When it comes to scaling a business with systems, few examples are as powerful as McDonald's. What set McDonald's apart in the early days wasn't its unique food but rather its unique approach to efficiency and automation. Ray Kroc, the driving force behind McDonald's expansion, understood that creating a streamlined system for every step of the food preparation process would allow McDonald's to consistently serve high-quality food quickly, regardless of location. By optimizing processes and reducing the need for specialized skills, McDonald's not only reduced costs but also became a globally recognized brand for speed and consistency.

This strategy allowed McDonald's to scale rapidly while maintaining a reliable customer experience. Just as McDonald's implemented efficient systems to become a global powerhouse, financial professionals can adopt systems to streamline operations, automate repetitive tasks, and focus on activities that fuel growth. Systems allow us to maximize efficiency, reduce stress, and increase productivity, ultimately freeing up more time for high-impact work.

The 80/20 Principle—Focusing on High-Impact Activities

The 80/20 Principle, popularized by Richard Koch in *The 80/20 Principle*, reveals that 80% of results come from just 20% of our efforts. Known as the Pareto Principle, this concept is transformative for business growth because it directs our attention to the highest-value activities—the tasks that truly drive results. In financial services, identifying and prioritizing these high-impact tasks can be the difference between stagnation and rapid growth.

For instance, handling routine inquiries or follow-ups manually can be a time sink. By automating these tasks, you reclaim valuable hours that can be directed toward activities with greater potential—like building relationships, developing content, or strategizing business growth. Identifying your top 20% of tasks that yield 80% of results can make your business more efficient, productive, and sustainable.

Example: You could use the 80/20 Principle by automating responses for common questions through email sequences or chatbots, allowing more time to focus on building meaningful client relationships and crafting a long-term strategy for growth.

My Journey to Automation—The Path to Six Figures

After one of my early videos went viral, I found myself with hundreds of leads coming in each week. At first, this was thrilling; every day, I was booking appointments and seeing steady growth in revenue. But soon, the manual process of responding to each inquiry and managing appointments became overwhelming. I had initially posted my number in my videos so that leads could reach out directly, but this "system" quickly proved unsustainable.

Realizing I needed to streamline, I began using automated tools to regain control of my time and energy. I set up a landing page to capture lead information and paired it with Calendly so that clients could self-schedule appointments. This small change was a game-changer, allowing clients to book calls without waiting for a response from me. I also built a website with essential information on Indexed Universal Life (IUL), an FAQ section, and a short video explaining IUL benefits. This setup empowered clients to educate themselves and minimized repetitive questions.

With these systems, I was able to hit the six-figure mark. Leads received timely responses, self-scheduling made the process easier for them, and I could focus on high-impact areas of my business. This automation allowed me to scale while maintaining a streamlined, consistent process.

The Power of a CRM—A Central Hub for Scaling Your Business

One of the most impactful changes in my business came from integrating a comprehensive Customer Relationship Management (CRM) system. A CRM does far more than just store client information—it serves as a one-stop shop for all client interactions, from lead tracking to follow-ups. This centralized platform streamlined my entire process, automating tasks, organizing client data, and ensuring nothing slipped through the cracks.

The CRM I use is tailored specifically to the insurance industry, featuring pre-built templates for landing pages, scheduling, and automated workflows. This all-in-one tool allowed me to consolidate all aspects of my client interactions in a single location, so I no longer needed multiple tools or spreadsheets. Here's what my CRM provides:

Key Features of My CRM:

- **Pre-Built Templates**: Ready-made landing pages and website templates designed for different insurance products save time and maintain a professional brand presence.

- **Automated Drip Campaigns**: Email and SMS drips keep leads engaged with timely, relevant content until they're ready to take the next step.

- **Appointment Scheduling**: Built-in scheduling eliminates the need for third-party tools, seamlessly booking clients directly from the CRM.

- **Tracking and Analytics**: Track email opens, link clicks, and overall engagement, so I can focus on leads that show genuine interest.

My CRM has become the backbone of my business, eliminating the need for multiple tools and consolidating all client interactions in one place. This setup saved countless hours each week, keeping me organized, efficient, and focused on high-impact client interactions.

If you are interested in using the same CRM I use, you can scan the QR code below for more information and a direct link to access it.

ManyChat—Automating Engagement on Instagram and Beyond

Automation doesn't end with scheduling and follow-ups—engaging with leads on social media can be a powerful automation tool as well. ManyChat is an AI-driven chatbot tool that can automate interactions on platforms like

Instagram, Facebook Messenger, and WhatsApp, allowing for immediate, personalized responses around the clock.

How I Use ManyChat on Instagram

ManyChat allows me to automate responses based on specific keywords in Instagram comments. For example, when I post about an upcoming webinar, I ask viewers to comment a particular keyword (like "INFO" or "SIGN UP") if they're interested. ManyChat detects these comments and automatically sends a direct message with a registration link for the webinar, a "how-to" video, or a link to book an appointment. This saves me from manually responding to every comment, streamlining my workflow and ensuring that every lead receives timely information.

Features and Benefits of ManyChat:

- **Automated Replies**: ManyChat instantly responds to common keywords, providing information, links, or next steps for leads without manual effort.

- **Lead Qualification**: The bot can ask a few pre-qualifying questions to gauge interest level, giving me a sense of how ready a client is before I reach out personally.

- **24/7 Engagement**: ManyChat keeps the conversation going, even when I'm offline, ensuring leads are engaged and informed without delay.

ManyChat, combined with a CRM, creates an efficient, responsive experience for leads, reducing workload and ensuring that clients receive personalized engagement regardless of the time or platform.

Solo.to—Simplifying Multiple Links for Social Media

For anyone with multiple resources to share—such as links to webinars, appointment scheduling, social profiles, and blog posts—Solo.to is an excellent solution. Think of Solo.to as a streamlined way to house all your important links on one easy-to-access page. This is especially useful for social media platforms like Instagram, where you're limited to a single link in your bio.

With Solo.to, you can create a branded link hub that includes all relevant resources, directing clients to everything they need in one place. Whether you're promoting a new blog post, sharing your latest video, or encouraging followers to book an appointment, Solo.to makes navigating multiple links effortless.

Benefits of Using Solo.to:

- **Centralized Access**: One link in your bio can lead to multiple resources, making it easier for followers to find what they're looking for.

- **Customizable Branding**: Solo.to allows you to brand your link page to align with your business, making it look cohesive and professional.

- **Tracking Capabilities**: Solo.to provides analytics to see which links are getting the most clicks, helping you understand what content resonates with your audience.

For financial professionals, Solo.to is a valuable tool to promote everything from educational resources to booking links, ensuring that clients can easily find the right tools at the right time.

Creating a Personal Website—Establishing Credibility and Educating Clients

In today's digital world, a personal website is essential for establishing credibility and positioning yourself as an authority. A website centralizes your brand, houses valuable resources, and offers clients a professional online hub where they can learn more about your expertise. Potential clients often check for an online presence before reaching out, so having a website is a competitive advantage.

Why a Personal Website is Important:

- **Builds Credibility**: A well-designed website establishes your authority and professionalism, making clients feel confident in your expertise.

- **Educates Clients**: Host videos, blog posts, and an FAQ section to help clients understand the services you offer, reducing repetitive questions.

- **Centralizes Information**: A website serves as a one-stop shop for everything from contact details to appointment scheduling and educational resources.

- **Increases Visibility**: A website increases your discoverability, allowing clients to engage with your content at their convenience.

A personal website not only builds your authority but also simplifies the client experience, providing a comprehensive resource that enhances your brand.

Putting It All Together—Systems That 10X Growth

Implementing the right systems frees up your time, reduces repetitive tasks, and directs your energy toward high-impact activities that drive growth. Here's a recap of the essential tools and strategies that have allowed me to scale my business effectively:

- **CRM**: The central hub for client management, appointment scheduling, and automated follow-ups.

- **ManyChat**: Automates engagement on social media, offering timely responses without manual effort.

- **Solo.to**: Organizes multiple links on a single page, providing followers easy access to diverse resources.

- **Landing Pages and Calendly**: Capture leads and simplify appointment scheduling, allowing clients to book their own time.

- **Personal Website**: Enhances credibility and acts as a comprehensive resource for clients to engage with your content and services.

With these tools, I've created a streamlined business model that maximizes efficiency, engages leads effectively, and allows me to focus on high-value interactions. This blend of automation and organization has been instrumental in scaling my business sustainably while delivering quality client experiences.

Reflection Exercise—Evaluating and Implementing Your Systems

1. **Identify Your Time-Consuming Tasks**: List out daily and weekly tasks. Which ones could be automated to free up time?

2. **Choose Your Core Tools**: Based on your business model, select the tools (CRM, landing pages, social media automation) that will benefit you most.

3. **Set Up Tracking**: For each tool, implement analytics or reporting features. Tracking your engagement and lead conversion will highlight what's working and where to adjust.

4. **Create a Schedule for System Maintenance**: Automation doesn't mean "set it and forget it." Regularly review and refine your systems to ensure they're still aligned with your business goals.

Quote for Reflection: *"The successful warrior is the average man, with laser-like focus."* — Bruce Lee

Building Efficiency into Your Path to Success

As you build your business, automation and streamlined systems will be the foundation that allows you to grow sustainably. By freeing up time spent on repetitive tasks, you'll be able to focus on delivering value, building client relationships, and scaling your business effectively. Remember, growth doesn't have to mean more hours—it means smarter processes that make room for what matters most.

With a commitment to efficiency, the right tools, and consistent review, you'll be well-equipped to 10X your sales and build a business that scales smoothly with minimal friction. Embrace these systems, refine them as you grow, and watch as they become the backbone of your path to lasting success.

SIX FIGURES IN 12 MONTHS

CHAPTER 8

Facebook and Instagram Ads—How to Generate Qualified Leads 24/7

The Power of Paid Ads—A Game-Changer for Lead Generation

Companies like Amazon, Apple, and Nike each invest billions annually in paid advertising, seeing it as essential to staying top-of-mind with consumers and driving consistent revenue growth. Amazon alone spent over $16.9 billion on digital ads in 2022, a strategy that fuels billions in revenue by ensuring its products appear at every stage of the buyer's journey—from initial interest to final purchase. Apple uses a similar approach, with paid ads playing a critical role in nurturing customer loyalty, which directly contributes to its record-breaking profits.

For financial professionals, this model underscores a crucial point: advertising isn't simply an expense—it's a strategic investment with tremendous upside potential. While some agents may feel hesitant to spend on paid ads, thinking of it as a cost, the reality is that the returns can be substantial. Even a modest annual investment of $10,000 to $20,000 in targeted ads can help agents cross the six-figure mark by delivering a steady pipeline of qualified leads. With smart ad spending, financial professionals can build visibility, foster trust, and connect with high-value clients ready for the solutions they offer. In today's competitive market, ads are a game-changer, creating consistent lead flow that frees agents to focus on serving clients and growing their business.

My Journey with Paid Leads and Mentorship

As someone who grew my business largely through organic content, I was fortunate to see rapid growth. My consistency and experience allowed my content to drive substantial lead flow without spending on ads. However, as my influence grew, I began mentoring agents, teaching them how to leverage social media. I noticed that despite attending training sessions, many agents struggled to put in the daily work required to achieve results through organic content alone. The truth is, generating leads organically requires time, creativity, and consistency.

Because of this, I started working with agents to help them generate leads through Facebook and Instagram ads, offering a way for them to sustain lead flow even if they weren't yet consistent with organic posting. These paid strategies allow agents to scale their business and avoid the trap of exhausting warm leads. For many agents, ads provide a stable, predictable lead source that would otherwise be difficult to achieve through organic efforts alone.

Why Investing in Ads Brings Consistent Lead Flow

In the financial services industry, two primary methods exist for generating leads: organically, through unpaid methods like social media, and through paid ads. One reason why so many agents leave the industry within their first year is that they quickly run out of warm leads and aren't prepared to invest in ads. But paid advertising is foundational for successful businesses in every field, helping to create demand, capture interest, and convert prospects into clients. For agents who want to scale to six-figure earnings, ads are a strategic investment. Running ads to a targeted audience not only provides qualified leads but also allows you to reach clients who are actively seeking solutions for their financial future. Ads create the consistent lead flow that helps stabilize growth, establish your reputation, and drive business success without exhausting personal contacts.

How Much to Invest in Ads for Consistent Growth

A common question agents ask is how much to allocate to advertising. A practical guideline is to dedicate around 10-20% of your revenue goal to ads. For instance, if your goal is $100,000, investing $10,000-$20,000 annually in ads can generate a steady stream of qualified leads ready for your services, creating a predictable and scalable income source.

Applying the L.A.P.S. Method from *Oversubscribed*

Daniel Priestly's *Oversubscribed* introduces the L.A.P.S. Method—Leads, Appointments, Presentations, and Sales—which helps maintain an active sales pipeline by ensuring a steady flow through each stage:

1. **Leads**: Generate a consistent stream of prospects via ads or organic content.

2. **Appointments**: Convert leads into consultations or bookings.

3. **Presentations**: Present your solutions to meet clients' financial needs.

4. **Sales**: Guide clients through the next steps to close the sale.

Paid ads provide a continuous flow of leads, ensuring your pipeline remains active and supporting long-term growth.

Selecting Videos That Convert—My Approach to Choosing Ad Content

One of the most effective ways to ensure an ad performs well is to choose content that has already resonated with your audience. When I select a video for an ad, I start by reviewing my highest-performing videos on social media—those with at least 300,000 views. These videos show that the message resonates with followers, making them strong candidates for ad campaigns.

Here's how I approach video selection:

- **Identify Top-Performing Content**: Look at videos with high engagement, views, and shares. Videos that resonate with your followers are more likely to convert as ads.

- **Test with a Small Budget**: For new ad campaigns, try each video with a $50 budget over a few days. If it performs well, increase the budget; if not, test another video.

- **Track Results and Refine**: Not every video will yield great results, so ongoing monitoring is essential. Tracking which videos convert helps you refine your ad strategy.

This approach minimizes risk by starting with content that's already proven. For beginners, using your most engaging content as a base is a good way to start while gaining insight into what your audience values most.

Leveraging Facebook and Instagram Ads for Sustainable Growth

Paid ads offer an excellent opportunity to scale lead generation by targeting your ideal audience with precision. Here are strategies to maximize the effectiveness of your ad campaigns:

1. **Audience Targeting**: Use Facebook and Instagram's advanced targeting options to reach people based on demographics, interests, and life events. For instance, targeting those who recently bought a home, had a child, or started a new job is often effective for life insurance.

2. **Create Compelling Visuals and Video Ads**: Video ads tend to perform exceptionally well on social media. Use high-quality, concise videos that

highlight the benefits of your services and grab attention immediately.

3. **Retargeting Ads**: Retargeting ads let you engage with individuals who've already shown interest by visiting your site or viewing your content. This keeps your brand top of mind and nurtures warm leads toward a decision.

4. **A/B Testing**: Experiment with different ad elements—such as visuals, copy, and CTAs—to identify what resonates most with your audience. A/B testing helps refine your approach and maximize your return on investment.

5. **Lead Capture Pages**: Direct ads to a landing page with a clear lead capture form. Offering something valuable, like a free guide or a financial planning checklist, encourages prospects to share their information, boosting conversions.

Starting with Ads as a Beginner—Keeping It Simple

If you're new to digital marketing, the learning curve can be steep. Simplifying your approach can make the process more manageable. Here's a beginner-friendly approach to getting started with ads:

1. **Create a Facebook Business Page**: A business page is essential for running ads and establishing a professional online presence.

2. **Choose a Modest Budget**: Start with a manageable budget, such as $50 for a few days, to test ad performance without risking too much.

3. **Monitor and Adjust**: Watch metrics like click-through rates and engagement to understand ad effectiveness. Adjust targeting, copy, or visuals as needed to improve results.

4. **Consider Working with a Lead Vendor**: For those just starting, outsourcing lead generation to a reputable vendor ensures a steady lead flow while you focus on sales. Check out www.digitlifeagent.com to explore quality lead options.

The Role of a CRM—Streamlining Lead Management and Follow-Up

Incorporating a CRM into your business is essential for managing leads from initial contact through conversion. With a CRM, all incoming leads from ads are automatically captured, allowing for timely follow-up and engagement.

The CRM I use provides an all-in-one solution, ideal for insurance professionals:

- **Pre-Built Templates**: Ready-made templates for landing pages, emails, and automated workflows tailored to different insurance products.

- **Automated Messaging**: Leads receive personalized messages right after they enter the system, adding a personal touch.

- **Integrated Scheduling**: Leads can schedule directly in my calendar, making it easier to manage appointments.

A CRM keeps leads organized, improves follow-up timing, and creates a seamless process that saves time and adds a professional touch to every interaction.

Building a Consistent, Scalable Lead Pipeline

Facebook and Instagram ads are powerful tools for generating qualified leads, providing a steady flow, and enhancing brand awareness. With strategic targeting, engaging content, and CRM integration, you can create a seamless lead generation and follow-up process that fuels business growth. Paid advertising enables you to focus on valuable client interactions and establish a consistent, scalable approach to growth.

By staying top-of-mind with potential clients and freeing up time for high-impact activities, ads allow you to scale your business sustainably and build a foundation for lasting success.

CHAPTER 9

Triple Your Income with a Higher Comp

Why Compensation Matters in Financial Services

In the financial services industry, your commission structure has a huge impact on your income potential. Often, new agents don't realize that a small difference in commission percentages can mean tens of thousands of dollars in income each year. While many agents assume their agency's compensation is standard, staying in a low-comp environment can hold you back from reaching your financial goals and limit your growth in the industry.

The commission level you receive—the percentage of each policy sale that you actually keep—is the key factor in determining your earnings. Unfortunately, too many agents unknowingly work under agencies offering lower-than-market rates, believing it's the norm. A higher compensation level doesn't just increase your income; it also provides the resources to grow your business faster, allowing you to reinvest in lead generation, systems, and training.

SIX FIGURES IN 12 MONTHS

My Journey from 25% Commission to 130%—and Beyond

When I started in financial services, I was earning 25% commission. I believed this was a good rate. Coming from a business background, 25% seemed like a fair return on investment, and the agency I was with emphasized its "systems" and "training" as some of the best in the industry. I didn't know I could negotiate or even consider other options, so I took their word for it.

A few months later, however, I received an unexpected call from an agent at another agency. She mentioned that they provided leads and, most notably, started agents at 50% commission. I was shocked. Here I was, working hard to build a book of business on 25% comp, and she was talking about earning double that from the start. For the first time, I realized that higher compensation was possible. But, out of loyalty, I turned her down, still convinced that my agency was the best.

The Game-Changing Offer That Transformed My Career

Fast-forward to 2022. By this time, I had posted a TikTok video that went viral, reaching hundreds of thousands of people. Among the viewers was an old friend with whom I had done business nearly two decades ago. After seeing my video, he reached out to reconnect and catch up. During our conversation, he asked the question I'd heard from other agents before: "Would you consider joining our team?" I was still loyal to my agency and initially brushed off the offer.

Then he made me an offer that stopped me in my tracks: "We can start you at 100% commission." I was floored. I thought 50% was a high commission, but 100%? It sounded almost too good to be true. That kind of opportunity was simply impossible to ignore, and I decided to make the switch. In my mind, it was a simple calculation: the same work for quadruple the compensation was an undeniable win.

What's more, my story didn't stop at 100%. Thanks to my production levels, within a few months, I was bumped up to 120%, and today, I'm earning 130%. For many agents, these levels may sound unreal, but the truth is that in the right agency with the right approach, you can even go as high as 145%.

Financial Services—The Highest-Paying Industry

Many agents are unaware that financial services is the highest-paying industry in the world, with earnings potential that far outpaces real estate and other fields. In financial services, not only can you earn exceptional commissions, but you're also not limited by location. While real estate agents are bound to a specific geographic area, financial agents can operate across state lines with non-resident licenses. In fact, there have been times when I was conducting business from overseas—closing deals and generating income while on the other side of the world. This flexibility is only possible when you're non-captive and working with multiple carriers.

With the right agency, a high compensation structure, and the freedom to operate as a non-captive agent, financial services can offer unmatched financial and lifestyle benefits. You don't need to be locked into a single location, and you can tap into an income source that operates around the clock.

Captive vs. Non-Captive Agencies—The Path to Greater Freedom

- **Captive Agencies**: Captive agents are restricted to selling only the products of their agency. While these setups often include support and training, they limit earning potential with lower commissions and fewer product options, restricting agents to a narrower client base.

- **Non-Captive Agencies**: Non-captive agents, by contrast, have the freedom to work with multiple carriers and access a broader range of products. This structure allows non-captive agents to prioritize clients' needs while maximizing their earnings, often starting with commissions between 50% and 100% and increasing based on production.

Switching to a non-captive agency allowed me to scale my business quickly. The freedom to choose from multiple carriers helped me provide clients with better options and higher-value solutions. For agents aiming to reach six-figure incomes, a non-captive setup offers unparalleled flexibility and growth potential.

Compensation Comparisons—Captive vs. Non-Captive Earnings

The earnings difference between captive and non-captive agencies can be substantial. Here's a simple comparison:

- **Captive Agent at 25%**: Selling a $1,000 annual premium policy earns $250.

- **Non-Captive Agent at 100%**: The same policy brings in $1,000.

- **High-Performing Non-Captive Agent at 130%**: Selling at 130% yields $1,300 for the same policy.

Over a year, with 50 policies, a captive agent would make $12,500, whereas a high-performing non-captive agent could make $65,000. With the right structure and a high commission rate, you're able to scale much faster and with higher earnings per policy.

My Advice: Know Your Options and Don't Settle

If you're satisfied with your current compensation plan and see clear growth potential, it might make sense to stay where you are. However, if you feel limited by low commissions or a captive structure, consider exploring alternatives. Many agents aren't aware that switching to a non-captive agency with competitive comp plans could double, triple, or quadruple their income.

For agents interested in learning more about non-captive options and high-comp structures, my team is here to help. Feel free to reach out by emailing info@digitallifeagent.com, and we'll discuss ways to optimize your earning potential.

Key Questions to Ask When Choosing a Higher Comp Plan

Before making a switch, here are critical questions to consider:

1. **What is the starting commission level?**
   Understanding the base rate helps clarify what you'll earn from the beginning and if there's room to grow.

2. **How high can my commission rate go?**
   Agencies often cap rates based on performance. Knowing the upper limit helps you gauge the agency's commitment to rewarding success.

3. **What support and resources are provided?**
   A higher commission doesn't mean sacrificing support. Ensure the agency offers the resources, training, and tools to help you grow.

4. **Are there production requirements?**
   Some agencies increase commission rates based on production volume. Understanding these requirements helps you set realistic goals.

5. **Am I captive or non-captive?**
   Consider the flexibility and range of products you'll be able to offer clients. A non-captive structure can provide greater freedom.

Your Path to Financial Freedom

Switching to a higher compensation plan and working with a non-captive agency was transformative for my career. It provided the income needed to grow my business, the flexibility to serve clients in multiple locations, and the ability to work with a variety of carriers. For agents committed to maximizing their earnings, understanding and optimizing compensation is the foundation of a sustainable, profitable career.

In financial services, the potential for growth is nearly unlimited. By choosing the right agency, structure, and compensation plan, you can unlock levels of income and freedom that would otherwise be out of reach. Remember, the best agency is one that values your work, rewards your achievements, and supports your goals. If you're in a place that offers this, build on it. But if you feel limited, don't hesitate to explore other opportunities.

SIX FIGURES IN 12 MONTHS

CHAPTER 10

Make Money First, Then Recruit

Why You Should Build Income Before Building an Agency

Recruiting and building an agency is one of the most effective ways to expand your business and multiply your income in financial services. Recruiting can increase your income tenfold, creating a stream of residual income as recruits generate revenue. However, it's most effective once you've proven your success and achieved solid, tangible results. Trying to recruit without first establishing financial success makes it challenging to attract motivated agents who will trust your guidance.

If you aren't yet consistently earning $5,000 to $10,000 monthly, focus first on building your income before actively recruiting. You don't need six figures to start bringing on new agents, but demonstrating a reliable income makes you more credible and attractive as a mentor. When people see your results, they're more likely to follow you because they can trust that your guidance leads to real outcomes.

Quote for Reflection: "People don't follow dreams; they follow proof."

Success attracts others, creating a natural draw for recruits who seek to achieve the same outcomes. In fact, a study by *Entrepreneur* magazine found that 92% of people are more likely to believe in a vision backed by tangible success. By prioritizing income generation, you create a powerful recruiting foundation.

My Journey—Why Results Matter in Recruiting

One of the reasons I was drawn to my current partner's opportunity was his proven track record of success. He and his team were already making significant income—some earning between $200,000 and $400,000 annually. Seeing their level of success reassured me that I was joining a team that knew how to win, and that confidence was key to my decision.

When I started earning substantial income myself, people began to reach out to me. I didn't have to actively recruit or convince anyone; they were naturally drawn to my results. This is likely why you're reading this book—I'm not sharing theories but real-life, proven strategies. I've even shared bank statements with those who doubted my success, and that evidence has been transformative in gaining trust. My results were not a fluke but the result of dedicated effort, demonstrating that anyone willing to put in the work can achieve similar outcomes.

Quote for Reflection: "Success breeds success." – Mia Hamm

When others see your results, they're naturally drawn to your momentum and eager to learn how they can achieve similar outcomes.

Moving in Silence—The Power of Results-Based Recruiting

When I decided to leave my initial agency, I didn't tell anyone, not even the person who first introduced me to the industry. My goal was to prove myself before bringing others along. I moved in silence, focusing on achieving results. Within my first 30 days at the new agency, I made $17,000.

Once I had the results, I reached out to my previous manager to share what I'd accomplished in just one month. He immediately decided to join me, and he soon began recruiting others to join. My results eliminated the need for convincing or pitching. The numbers spoke for themselves.

Quote for Reflection: "Work hard in silence, let your success make the noise." – Frank Ocean

There's significant power in letting your results be the recruiting tool. Rather than convincing others with words, your earnings and progress make the case, attracting individuals ready to work toward similar success.

Money and Success Attract People Naturally

One of the main reasons I struggled in my first six months was the pressure to recruit without any financial results. Recruiting without income didn't make sense to me; as a business-minded person, I knew people follow results, not promises. According to a survey by Business Insider, 84% of professionals are more likely to follow a leader with proven success than one without a clear track record. This statistic reflects an important truth: people want to be led by someone who's already financially successful, not someone who's trying to teach them about money while struggling themselves.

Quote for Reflection: "Success attracts success, and failure attracts failure because of the law of attraction." – Rhonda Byrne

It's important to surround yourself with financially successful people, as they set a standard of excellence. People are inspired by leaders who walk the talk, not just talk about it. This is why focusing on your success first is crucial before expanding your reach through recruiting.

Key Benefits of Recruiting After Achieving Financial Success

1. **Enhanced Credibility**: A proven track record makes people trust you, increasing the likelihood that recruits will follow your guidance and work hard under your mentorship.

2. **Magnetic Attraction**: When you're successful, people naturally gravitate toward you, wanting to learn your strategies and mirror your results.

3. **Residual Income**: Building a team amplifies your earning potential, generating a stream of income from each agent's success.

4. **Increased Influence**: Financial success builds your reputation, allowing you to influence and attract higher-quality recruits who are committed to their success.

5. **Easier Recruiting**: With your own success as proof, potential recruits need less convincing. Your income serves as the "presentation" that attracts them to join your team.

Key Questions to Ask Yourself Before Recruiting

If you're considering building an agency, assess your readiness by asking these questions:

1. **Have I established a consistent income level?** Are you generating income that shows you understand how to make money in this industry?

2. **Am I a credible example of success for others?** Can recruits look at your journey and see proof of what's possible if they follow your guidance?

3. **Do I have a proven strategy I can share?**
   Have you developed methods that others can follow, or are you still figuring things out yourself?

4. **Do I have the time and energy to mentor others effectively?**
   Recruiting isn't just about numbers; it requires dedication to mentorship. Can you balance your own workload with the responsibility of guiding others?

5. **Am I prepared to support recruits through the learning curve?**
   Success in financial services has ups and downs. Are you equipped to help new recruits navigate the challenges of the industry?

Build Your Foundation Before Recruiting

Building income before actively recruiting is not only beneficial for your own growth but also strengthens your credibility as a leader. When you achieve tangible results, recruiting becomes a natural extension of your success. Success attracts people, and by prioritizing financial results, you set yourself up for more impactful and effective recruiting.

Quote for Reflection: "You don't have to chase people. If you're successful, they will chase you." – Grant Cardone

In this industry, establishing a track record isn't just advantageous—it's essential. Your foundation of financial success will draw the right people to you, making it easier to scale your agency with motivated and committed recruits.

SIX FIGURES IN 12 MONTHS

CHAPTER 11

How to Stay Ahead of the Competition

Learning from the Leaders—How Apple Stays Ahead in a Fierce Market

When it comes to staying ahead of the competition, Apple is a prime example. Known for groundbreaking innovation, Apple doesn't just react to market demands—it defines them. From launching the first iPhone to creating a seamless ecosystem with devices like the Apple Watch and AirPods, Apple's approach goes beyond just selling products; it's about building a brand that anticipates and fulfills consumer needs before they even realize they have them. Apple invests billions in research and development each year, constantly innovating, even when they're already at the top. Why? Because they know that fierce competition is always waiting in the wings, ready to capitalize on any slowdown or misstep.

This constant drive to stay ahead requires Apple to evolve, find new ways to serve its customers, and retain its reputation as a leader in tech. The tech industry moves fast, with competitors like Samsung and Google closely following Apple's moves. To maintain their position, Apple consistently pushes the boundaries, not just in technology but also in branding and customer experience, keeping their loyal customer base engaged while attracting new users.

As financial professionals, we can take a similar approach by always innovating and staying one step ahead of industry trends. Just as Apple reinvents the way people experience technology, we can create new ways to connect with clients, stand out from the crowd, and expand our reach.

My Journey of Evolving Strategies

In my own career, staying ahead has meant constantly looking for ways to differentiate myself in an industry that's increasingly competitive. When I started out in 2021, very few agents were discussing Indexed Universal Life (IUL) policies or creating educational content around them. I leaned into this space early and built a strong reputation for myself, but as I saw more and more agents entering the market with similar messaging, I realized that standing out would require fresh strategies.

One of the best ways I find inspiration for new approaches is by attending events with high-income earners. Each time I go, I learn something new—something that elevates my business. Recently, I attended a two-day training event for life insurance agents, where I was invited to serve as a trainer and panelist. During one session, a speaker was discussing how she built her business by focusing solely on her warm market. Her approach was different from the traditional warm market approach, and it immediately caught my attention.

This agent was originally from Kenya and had focused her business on educating Kenyans about life insurance and financial strategies. Her primary product was IUL, just like mine. However, rather than starting there, she led with term policies, which were more accessible and relatable to her community. Then, during her client meetings, she assessed their financial status and needs to see if an IUL would be a good fit. Her process was structured, allowing her to introduce term policies as an entry point and later transition qualifying clients to more comprehensive IUL plans.

Hearing her story, my mind immediately started turning with possibilities. If she could do this in her community, I could tailor a similar strategy to my own background and experience with Nigerians in the diaspora. It was a lightbulb moment, and I knew I could apply this approach in a way that would resonate with my community.

The "$100 for $1 Million" Campaign

Inspired by this conversation, I created a campaign specifically for the Nigerian diaspora called the "$100 for $1 Million" campaign. The concept was simple: many people in my community were unfamiliar with life insurance, so I wanted to show them how it could be a valuable wealth-building tool. Through the campaign, I explained that, depending on age and gender, they could secure a million-dollar term policy for as little as $100 per month. You can check out www.secureafricanfamilies.com to learn more about the campaign.

Now, you might be thinking, "But Dipo, I thought your focus was on permanent life insurance policies, like IULs?" That's true—99% of my business revolves around IULs. However, as a business owner, sometimes you have to think outside the box to reach new audiences. This campaign allowed me to connect with clients who might not otherwise consider life insurance. Once they were in the door, I could conduct a full financial analysis. Based on their income, assets, and financial goals, I could then discuss options like an IUL or even an annuity if it made sense for them.

This campaign gave me a unique way to reach my community, address their financial concerns, and build trust. By targeting an underrepresented group with a tailored message, I differentiated myself from other agents and expanded my reach. The strategy was more than just a campaign—it was a way to make life insurance relatable and accessible to a community that had previously been underserved.

Tips for Staying Ahead of the Competition

In this industry, maintaining a competitive edge requires agility, curiosity, and a willingness to continuously evolve your strategies. Here are some ways to stay ahead:

1. **Invest in Ongoing Education**: Digital marketing, social media, and even financial products are always evolving. Staying current on industry trends, tools, and best practices is essential for remaining relevant. Make it a habit to read industry publications, take courses, and attend training sessions.

2. **Attend Events and Network with High Performers**: One of the best ways to learn new strategies is by networking with successful people. Attending industry events, training sessions, and conferences gives you a chance to hear new perspectives, gain insights, and apply what you've learned. By connecting with high-income earners, you get a first-hand look at what's working and what's not, allowing you to bring fresh ideas into your own business.

3. **Experiment and Innovate**: Don't be afraid to try new methods and platforms to reach your target audience. Whether it's using video content on TikTok, hosting virtual financial workshops, or creating email newsletters, experimenting with different approaches can help you identify what resonates most with your clients.

4. **Target Specific Communities or Professions**: Like my "$100 for $1 Million" campaign, finding an underserved group can set you apart. Think about how you can tailor your messaging to resonate with specific audiences. For example, you could focus on teachers nearing retirement, nurses who may need income protection, or young professionals interested in building wealth early on.

5. **Leverage Automation and Systems**: Efficiency is key to scaling. Use CRM systems, automation, and content scheduling tools to stay organized, freeing up time to focus on high-value activities like closing

sales and developing client relationships. Automation helps you stay top of mind with clients without taking up valuable hours each day.

Questions to Spark Creative Ideas

Here are some questions to help you brainstorm ways to stay ahead in your business:

- What common financial concerns or misconceptions exist in my target market?

- Are there specific communities or demographics that could benefit from targeted financial education?

- How can I use my personal background, interests, or unique skills to connect more deeply with my audience?

- Are there ways to reframe or package traditional products in a way that feels fresh, engaging, or more relatable?

Staying Agile and Focused on Growth

As the financial services industry becomes more competitive, staying agile and willing to adapt is crucial. The market will continue to shift, and new agents will enter the space, but those who continually evolve will remain successful. In my journey, I've found that flexibility, curiosity, and a drive to stay ahead have been instrumental in reaching my goals.

Whether it's by launching a new campaign, learning from high-performing agents, or targeting specific communities, the strategies that keep you agile and relevant will help you grow a sustainable, profitable business. Staying one step ahead is not about reinventing the wheel; it's about finding ways to make your message resonate in fresh, impactful ways.

SIX FIGURES IN 12 MONTHS

CHAPTER 12

Imitate the Top 10% of Agents

The Power of Imitation—Learning from the Masters

In *Richer, Wiser, Happier* by William Green, there's a remarkable story about Mohnish Pabrai, an investor who credits much of his success to a simple, yet powerful approach: imitation. Pabrai, who deeply admired Warren Buffett's investing style, decided that instead of forging his own path, he would study and imitate Buffett's every move. Pabrai spent years analyzing Buffett's philosophy, watching his speeches, and dissecting his investments. Eventually, Pabrai went as far as bidding over $600,000 for a private lunch with Buffett to gain first-hand insights. He understood that even one transformative conversation could multiply his success many times over.

Pabrai explained, *"If you want to accomplish something, it's wise to figure out the best that's been done and do it even better."* Rather than trying to create an entirely new approach, Pabrai chose to emulate someone who was already achieving extraordinary results. This mindset is a direct shortcut to success and an example of how powerful mentorship and imitation can be in one's journey. In our field, it's no different. The most successful agents have learned what works, and mentorship allows us to benefit from their years of experience, without having to endure the same costly mistakes.

Why Investing in Mentorship is Essential

Success is a journey that's significantly accelerated by guidance from those who have already traveled it. Top achievers in any field possess insights and strategies they've gained through years of experience. These are often lessons that books and traditional training programs simply can't provide. Mohnish Pabrai invested over $600,000 for a lunch with Buffett, recognizing the high return on investment that comes with mentorship. That price was not just for a meal, but for decades' worth of wisdom.

The American Society for Training and Development reports that individuals with mentors are five times more likely to experience success in their field than those who go it alone. Mentorship can make a massive difference in both your confidence and your strategy. For me, mentorship was a game-changer. As a new agent, I started off in an environment where agents around me had years of experience but were barely making ends meet. They were following outdated methods, didn't have the tools for lead generation, and were resigned to struggling for every sale. Staying in that environment would have severely limited my potential.

Quote for Reflection: "Success leaves clues." – Tony Robbins

My Turning Point—Learning from High-Earning Agents

The breakthrough came when I transitioned to a new agency where success was the standard. Here, $10,000 a month wasn't even impressive; it was simply the minimum expectation. The environment was transformative. I became committed to learning directly from these top earners and took every opportunity to join training calls, travel to events, and even invest thousands of dollars to gain access to these leaders' insights. I didn't need anyone to hold my hand— I'm self-motivated and a natural go-getter—but I knew that simply being in the room with high performers would provide invaluable knowledge.

Every time I picked up a new strategy, I implemented it immediately. I didn't wait or second-guess; I trusted in the value of what I was learning. **Eighty percent of the success strategies you've read about in this book** are a result of me applying what I learned from these high-earning mentors.

One of my most powerful breakthroughs came from watching a top agent who had over a million followers on TikTok. I noticed he posted a video on why people don't have life insurance, and it went viral. Inspired, I thought, *"What if I adapt this idea with my own spin and see if it resonates?"* I wasn't even focused on generating leads initially; I was just testing the waters. Sure enough, the video went viral, drawing thousands of views and transforming my business overnight. That moment was a testament to the power of imitation. All I did was emulate a strategy that was already successful for someone else, adding my own voice and perspective.

The Proven Path to Success—Mentorship and Replication

Today, I mentor agents across the country and teach them the same principles, strategies, and techniques that have fueled my growth. My mentorship program focuses on empowering agents to follow in the footsteps of success. One thing I've noticed repeatedly is that those who commit to implementing the strategies I teach consistently see results. This is the power of mentorship and imitation in action—it's about leveraging the experience of those who've walked the path before you.

Quote for Reflection: "If you want to accomplish something, it's wise to figure out the best that's been done and do it even better." – Mohnish Pabrai

The top performers in any field don't achieve their status through luck; they develop routines, systems, and mindsets that anyone can replicate if they're willing to learn and apply themselves. In this industry, you don't have to reinvent the wheel to succeed. You just need to recognize a good wheel, get into it, and roll forward with it.

Tips for Finding the Right Mentor

Investing in mentorship is one of the most impactful steps toward accelerating your career, but finding the right mentor requires discernment. Here's how to identify the best fit:

1. **Look for Results, Not Just Experience**: Years in the industry don't always equal success. Seek a mentor with a track record of real results in the areas you want to excel in. Ensure their achievements align with your goals.

2. **Be Willing to Invest**: Valuable mentorship often requires a financial commitment. Be prepared to invest in your mentor's programs or sessions. Remember, the knowledge and insights you gain can yield a tremendous return on investment when applied correctly.

3. **Find Compatibility**: A mentor's values and approach should resonate with you. The best mentorship relationships happen when you respect and relate to your mentor's way of working, making it easier to implement their advice with full commitment.

4. **Observe, Imitate, and Adapt**: Observe your mentor's strategies and processes closely. Imitation isn't about losing your individuality—it's about applying a framework that's already proven successful. Adapt it to your own style, audience, and goals.

According to *Forbes*, professionals who seek mentorship often earn 20-30% more over their careers than those who don't. This potential for growth makes mentorship an invaluable investment for agents committed to excelling in their field.

A Quick Summary and Your Call to Action

Throughout this book, I've shared strategies, insights, and personal experiences designed to empower you in achieving six-figure success in the life insurance industry. We've explored the power of building a personal brand, utilizing social media, automating your business, and selecting the right agency to maximize your earnings. Now, it's up to you to turn this knowledge into action.

If there's one key takeaway from this book, it's that success in the life insurance industry is within reach if you're willing to apply proven methods, seek guidance from those who've succeeded before you, and invest in your own growth. Emulate the best practices of those who are already where you want to be, adapt their methods to suit your style, and seek mentorship along the way.

So, here's my challenge to you: Start today. Implement these insights, find a mentor who resonates with you, and take calculated risks. The life insurance industry offers unlimited potential for those willing to learn and grow.

Remember, the top 10% didn't get there by accident—they followed a path to success that you now have the tools to follow, too.

I look forward to seeing you at the top.

SIX FIGURES IN 12 MONTHS

SIX FIGURES IN 12 MONTHS

References

Chapter 1
- Roger Bannister: The 4-Minute Mile and Its Legacy," *BBC Sport*, 2014.

Chapter 3
- Feldman, Ben. *The Feldman Method: A Sales Guide for Insurance and Financial Professionals*, 1969.
- Kim, W. Chan, and Mauborgne, Renée. *Blue Ocean Strategy: How to Create Uncontested Market Space and Make the Competition Irrelevant*, 2005.
- Sullivan, Dan, and Hardy, Benjamin. *10X is Easier Than 2X: How World-Class Entrepreneurs Achieve More by Doing Less*, 2023.

Chapter 6
- Katz, Donald. *Just Do It: The Nike Spirit in the Corporate World*, 1994.
- Hennessy, Brittany. *Influencer: Building Your Personal Brand in the Age of Social Media*, 2018.
- Johnson, Michael. *Branding: In Five and a Half Steps*, 2016.
- Godin, Seth. *This is Marketing: You Can't Be Seen Until You Learn to See*, 2018.

Chapter 7
- Kroc, Ray, and Anderson, Robert. *Grinding It Out: The Making of McDonald's*, 1977.
- Koch, Richard. *The 80/20 Principle: The Secret to Achieving More with Less*, 1997.
- Collier, Robert. *The Secret of the Ages*, 1926.

Chapter 8
- "Amazon, Apple, and Nike: How They Use Advertising to Stay Dominant," *MarketingWeek*, 2022.

Chapter 12
- Green, William. *Richer, Wiser, Happier: How the World's Greatest Investors Win in Markets and Life*, 2021.

… SIX FIGURES IN 12 MONTHS

SIX FIGURES IN 12 MONTHS

Made in the USA
Middletown, DE
15 November 2024